BEAR & ALLIGATOR T·A·L·E·S

Real Bears and Alligators

By Fay Robinson

Illustrations by Ann Iosa

ⓒP CHILDRENS PRESS®

CHICAGO

Photo Credits

© ANIMALS ANIMALS—© C. C. Lockwood, 20; © Ted Levin, 22 (top)

© JERRY HENNEN—13, 27

© JAMES P. ROWAN—12, 16, 23 (top)

© TOM STACK & ASSOCIATES—© Thomas Kitchin, 5, 17; © Richard P. Smith, 7 (bottom left), 22 (bottom); © E.P.I. Nancy Adams, 25

SUPERSTOCK INTERNATIONAL, INC.—© Mia and Klaus, 7 (bottom right)

VALAN—© Wayne Lankinen, 15

VISUALS UNLMITED—© Glenn Oliver, 4, 7 (top right); © Nada Pecnik, 6, 21; © Ron Spomer, 7 (top left); © John D. Cunningham, 8; © Tom Edwards, 9, 18, 29; © John Serrao, 10; © William J. Weber, 11; © Kirtley-Perkins, 14; © Science Visuals Unlimited, 19; © WIll Troyer, 23 (bottom); © Valorie Hodgson, 24; © Dick Poe, 26; © Milton H. Tierney, Jr., 28

ANN IOSA—Art, Cover, 2, 3, 30

Library of Congress Cataloging-in-Publication Data

Robinson, Fay.
    Real bears and alligators / by Fay Robinson : illustrated by Ann Iosa.
      p. cm. — (Bear and alligator tales)
    Summary: Bear and Alligator, two stuffed toys, compare the characteristics and habits of the black bear and the American alligator.
    ISBN 0-516-02374-8
    1. Black bear—Juvenile literature. 2. American alligator—Juvenile literature. [1. Alligators. 2. Black bear. 3. Bears.] I. Iosa, Ann, ill. II. Title. III. Series: Robinson, Fay. Bear and alligator tales.
QL737.C27R59   1992
597.98—dc20
                                           92-10755
                                             CIP
                                           AC

Bear and Alligator were looking
at books.

"Alligators are better than bears,
you know," said Alligator.

"Bears are just as good," said Bear.

"We'll see," said Alligator.

Alligators are long and thin.

Bears are round and heavy.

Alligators are usually gray.

Bears are lots of colors—

black,

brown,

brownish-red,

white.

Alligators have thick, tough skin.

Bears have thick, furry coats.

Alligators live where the weather is warm.

They mostly live in swamps.

Bears live where the weather is colder.
They mostly live in forests.

Alligators spend most of their
time in the water.

Bears spend
most of their
time on land.
They also
climb trees.

Alligators hatch from eggs.
Usually around 35 babies hatch
at one time.

Bears are born live. Usually two babies are born at one time.

Baby alligators are sometimes called barkers. But most of the time they are just called baby alligators.

Baby bears are always called cubs.

Alligators have lots of sharp teeth.

So do bears!

Alligators love to eat fish.

So do bears!

Alligators also eat bugs and
small animals—like turtles.

Bears also eat bugs,
animals, and plants.

Alligators like to lie around.
So do bears!

But alligators run very quickly
when they need to.

So do
bears!

Alligators swim very well.

So do bears!

Alligators roar very loudly.

So do bears!

"Do you still think alligators are better than bears?" asked Bear.

"Bears are better than I thought," said Alligator. "But I'm glad I'm an alligator."

"Well, that's good because I'm glad I'm a bear," said Bear.

About the Author

Fay Robinson received a bachelor's degree in Child Study from Tufts University and a master's degree in Education from Northwestern University. She has taught preschool and elementary children and is the author of several picture books.

About the Artist

Ann Iosa received her professional training at Paier School of Art in New Haven, Connecticut. Her illustrations have appeared in numerous children's books, as well as in several popular magazines. Ann lives with her husband and two children in Southbury, Connecticut.